CONTENTS

FOREWORD

History is so much more than just a boring collection of names and dates. It is a collection of stories—sometimes tragic stories, sometimes heroic stories, sometimes romantic stories, sometimes scary stories. And they're all stories of real people who lived real lives.

Those stories can get lost in the shuffle of memorizing battles, studying maps, and listing important court cases or rulers. That's why primary sources are so valuable. They remind us that historical events happened to and because of real people. Reading diaries, looking at photographs, and seeing newspaper articles are just some ways to make history feel personal through primary sources.

Another way is through watching or listening to interviews with people who lived through major historical events. That's what you're invited to do in this book—and all the books that are part of the *Rosen Publishing Primary Source Library*. Each chapter includes quotes from an interview with a real person who experienced a major historical event in a deeply personal way. You can also scan the QR code included at the beginning of each chapter to watch a video interview with the person featured in that chapter.

Created in partnership with Generations Broadcasting, the *Rosen Publishing Primary Source Library* was created to remind readers that there is power in sharing our stories. First-person stories make history come alive. And when history comes alive, we're better able to learn from it—and avoid the mistakes of the past.

The events you're living through today will be part of the next generation's history lessons. As you read and watch the stories collected here, think about what you want your story to be.

Note: More interviews about the topics featured in this series, as well as many other historical events, can be accessed via a subscription to Rosen Publishing's GBC Stories Database: rosendigital.com/GBCStories/.

HOW TO WATCH THE INTERVIEWS FEATURED IN THIS BOOK

- Use your phone's camera, and hold it over the QR code.
- Click the link that appears.
- Watch the video that pops up. If you would like to read a transcript of the interview while you watch, you can click on that option in the video's menu.

INTRODUCTION

On December 7, 1941, Japan launched a surprise **aerial** attack on a U.S. naval base at Pearl Harbor on Oahu Island in Hawai'i. The attack led to the United States joining World War II (1939–1945). While the attack was a surprise, it came after years of **tension** between the United States and Japan that was impossible to **resolve**.

Japan tried to **negotiate** with the United States up until the day of the attack on Pearl Harbor, when Japan's prime minister, Tōjō Hidecki declared war with the attack. Planning for the **assault** on the naval base began in November, but it was made clear that the attack could be canceled. However, on November 26, Vice Admiral Nagumo Chuichi led six aircraft carriers, three cruisers, two battleships, and eleven destroyers to approximately 275 miles (440 km) north of Hawai'i. From this point, they launched 360 planes for the assault on Pearl Harbor.

About 100 U.S. naval vessels and 8 battleships were stationed at Pearl Harbor. Admiral Edward Kimmel and Lieutenant General Walter C. Short led the command at Pearl Harbor and were warned as early as October 1941 that there was a possibility of an act of war and to start an appropriate defensive **deployment**.

However, the measures that were taken weren't enough and left the northwest area around Pearl Harbor, which was the area that made the most sense for an attack, undefended. No one seriously believed that Pearl Harbor itself would be the target of an attack.

On the morning of Sunday, December 7, officials in Washington, D.C., learned that Japan wanted a meeting with the secretary of state at 1:00 p.m. (this would have been 7:30 a.m. in Pearl Harbor). The message was a sign that war was likely. However, the message took a while to decode, and the U.S. Army chief of staff, George C. Marshall, was horseback riding at the time, which meant the message wasn't seen until 11:15 a.m. in Washington, D.C.

Marshall sent a warning to the naval officers at Pearl Harbor, but sent it by telegram instead of by phone because he was worried the message would be intercepted. The telegram wasn't filed until noon, an hour before the attack. An additional mix-up in

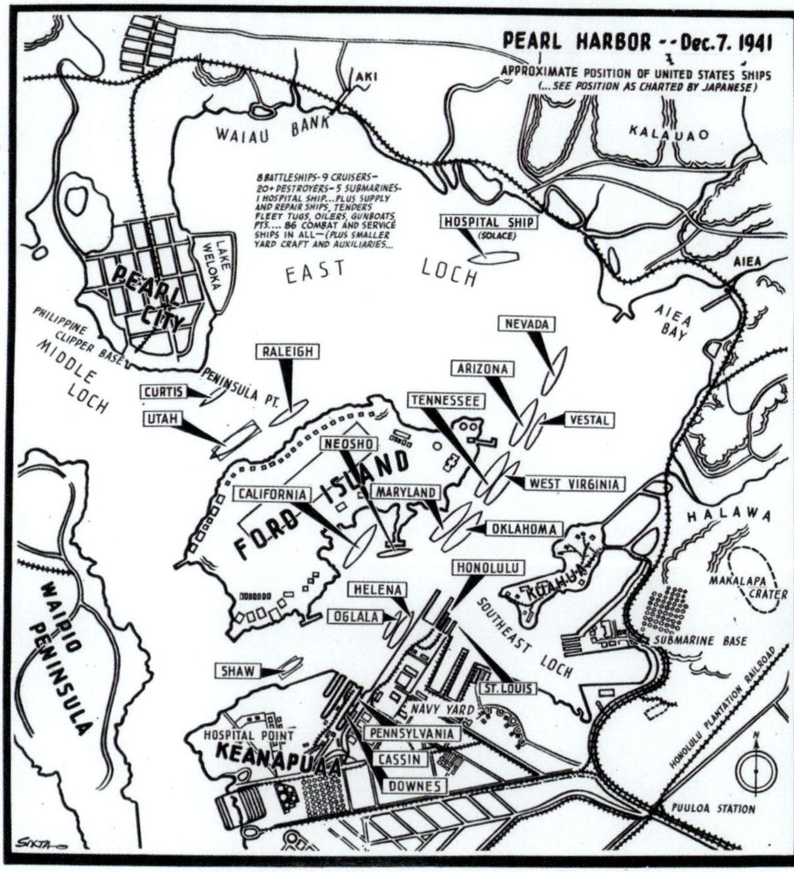

This map shows Pearl Harbor and where the battleships were lined up in Battleship Row on December 7, 1941.

communication meant that this telegram wasn't even received in Hawai'i until the attack had already started.

The attack started at 7:55 a.m. with the first wave of 200 Japanese torpedo planes, fighters, and bombers. The second wave started at 8:50 a.m. but was not as successful as the first wave. The overall attack ended just after 9:00 a.m. While it did not last long, it made a huge impact. The attack took the lives of more than 2,400 Americans and destroyed hundreds of aircraft and several battleships in what was called Battleship Row.

President Franklin D. Roosevelt called it "a date which will live in infamy." The attack changed people's minds about staying neutral in World War II. On December 8, the United States voted to declare war on Japan, officially entering the war and, with it, a new era in U.S. history.

CHAPTER ONE

THE UNITED STATES MOVES TOWARD WAR

By the late 1930s, trouble was spreading throughout the world. In Europe, Adolf Hitler's Nazi Germany was invading nearby countries and starting what would become World War II, which began in 1939. Meanwhile, in Asia, Japan was taking control of parts of China and looking toward Southeast Asia for further expansion. Among all this, the United States had adopted a stance of neutrality, but many people wondered if the nation could stay out of the conflict forever.

For young men **enlisting** in the U.S. military at the time, the future felt uncertain. Many had not traveled far from home or even seen the ocean. No one knew where exactly their base would be once they enlisted, especially with the war in Europe getting more dangerous. This was a concern of Jim's, who was interviewed about his time in the military during the bombing of Pearl Harbor. Jim, like many others, hoped for assignments in quiet areas that seemed safe from world events.

RECEIVING A FLEET ASSIGNMENT

Jim was one of thousands of young men who joined the military during this time and **anxiously** awaited his base

Scan this QR code to watch Jim describe how he turned 18 and celebrated with a luau and then later woke up to explosions from Pearl Harbor being attacked.

This photo from a Japanese aircraft shows the early stages of the attack on Pearl Harbor. A torpedo can be seen hitting the water.

assignment. The fighting in Europe was becoming more **intense**, and Jim worried he'd be sent into the heart of the danger. He said:

> *[I] graduated from Tool and Die Maker School; [then] we received our ... assignment to the fleet. We didn't know where we were going ... The war in Europe was really getting hot. I didn't relish the idea of going to the Atlantic fleet because it looked like that's where all the stuff was gonna hit the fan ... I got my orders to go to Pearl Harbor ... I couldn't*

FAST FACT

PEARL HARBOR WAS THE MAIN BASE FOR THE U.S. PACIFIC FLEET. IT HOUSED MANY AIRCRAFT, THOUSANDS OF SERVICE MEMBERS, AND DOZENS OF BATTLESHIPS ALONG BATTLESHIP ROW.

The attacks destroyed military aircraft that were essential to helping defend the harbor.

FAST FACT

MOST OF THE U.S. BATTLESHIPS THAT WERE DAMAGED IN THE ATTACK ON PEARL HARBOR WERE REPAIRED, EXCEPT FOR THE USS *ARIZONA*, WHICH SANK AND IS STILL BELOW THE OCEAN, THE USS *UTAH*, WHICH SANK AND COULD NOT BE SALVAGED, AND THE USS *OKLAHOMA*, WHICH WAS TOO DAMAGED AND SANK ON ITS WAY TO CALIFORNIA FOR SCRAPPING IN 1947.

get farther away from harm in Pearl Harbor, Hawai'i.

Hawai'i seemed like the calmest place that Jim could possibly be stationed. It was more than 2,000 miles (3,218.6 km) from the U.S. mainland and even farther from Europe and Asia. It seemed like the last place anyone would expect war to strike.

CLOSE TO WAR

In Pearl Harbor, the weather was warm all year, the beaches and coastline were beautiful, and palm trees lined the roads. For many, it was the perfect posting since it was far from the battlefields of Europe and growing tensions in Asia. However, Japan and theUnited States were moving closer to conflict.

FAST FACT

BEFORE 1941, JAPAN RECEIVED ABOUT 80 PERCENT OF ITS OIL FROM THE UNITED STATES. WHEN THE SHIPMENTS STOPPED, JAPAN ONLY HAD ENOUGH FOR ABOUT TWO YEARS OF WAR.

The USS *West Virginia* and USS *Tennessee* are shown here during the attack on Pearl Harbor.

WHY JAPAN ATTACKED PEARL HARBOR

Japan and the United States were becoming rivals years before the attack on Pearl Harbor, even though they hadn't gone to war yet. Japan was trying to take greater control over the Pacific region and wanted more natural resources like oil and rubber.

In 1937, open warfare started between Japan and China, and in response, the U.S. government gave its first loan to China in 1938. Following this, the United States ended the 1911 Treaty of **Commerce** and **Navigation** with Japan in 1939. In 1940, the United States started **restricting** the **exports** of materials that were useful in war, such as oil, to Japan.

Tensions continued to increase between the United States and Japan, and by summer 1941, Japan entered an **alliance** with Germany and Italy (also known as the Axis powers). In response to this, the United States cut off all financial relations with Japan, and shipments of petroleum and other war materials were prevented from being shipped to Japan.

Meanwhile, in Japan, people in the government were upset over the loan the U.S. provided to China. The United States and Japan tried to come to an understanding, but when it became clear that wasn't possible, Japan attacked Pearl Harbor.

Japan's goal was to attack before the United States had a chance to respond and were least expecting it, which is why they attacked early on a Sunday morning. They wanted to destroy American

Japan had been fighting in China since the early 1930s and wanted more control in the Pacific region as well as the resources this control would give them, such as oil and coal.

The United States tried to slow Japan down by limiting what American companies could sell to them, especially oil. Japan relied heavily on oil for its ships, planes, and military factories. When the United States stopped providing oil to Japan, its leaders saw this as a threat.

A wrecked Japanese plane is shown here.

battleships and airplanes, hoping that this would prevent the United States from interfering with Japan's expansion into Southeast Asia. Instead, the attack pushed the United States into World War II.

SUNDAY MORNING ATTACK

The night before the attack on Pearl Harbor, Jim celebrated his birthday and went to a luau at Cooley Beach, enjoying the food, music, and dancing. He went to sleep that night, unaware of what awaited him, and woke to the sound of explosions:

> *I got a ride down to the Navy yard gate. The torpedo run had already occurred, and Battleship Row was [filling with] black smoke. Planes were still* ***strafing*** *in the harbor. When I entered the Navy yard, just as I got back to*

An aerial photo of the first wave of the attack is shown here.

the ship ... we were hit with a 500-pound [227 kg] bomb; it ruptured our hull and flooded one of our magazines. But we had no loss of life. We were waiting for the other shoe to drop.

On Sunday morning at 7:55 a.m. in Pearl Harbor, the first wave of 200 torpedo planes, fighters, and bombers appeared, immediately starting a vicious attack. Many U.S. military planes were packed tightly on Ford Island, as well as at Wheeler and Hickam fields, and many of these aircraft were destroyed while still on the ground. At Wheeler field, 42 out of 126 planes were destroyed, and 41 were damaged, which left only 43 able to be used. Only six airplanes were able to make it into the air during the first wave of the attack.

At the same time as the airplanes on the ground were destroyed, Japanese bombers were also attacking ships in the harbor. Because it was Sunday morning, the ships weren't fully manned, which left them vulnerable.

ON THE FRONT LINES

The attack destroyed and damaged battleships in minutes. USS *Arizona* was hit by multiple bombs, leading to a massive explosion and sinking, killing 1,177 crew members. The USS *West Virginia* was struck by seven torpedoes and two bombs. More than 100 lives were lost on the USS *West Virginia*. The USS *Oklahoma* was hit by four torpedoes within five minutes, which made it

The USS *Arizona* is shown here sinking after being hit during the air attack.

Some ships, like the USS *Shaw*, were able to be repaired to return to duty even though it experienced significant damage. The USS *Shaw*'s forward magazine exploded, but was repaired and served in World War II.

capsize and trapped hundreds of sailors on the ship. Rescue efforts saved 32 men, but 429 died. The USS *California* and USS *Utah* were also torpedoed and sunk.

Some ships, like Jim's, suffered minor damage and were repaired in time to return to duty. Jim discussed how foolish it was that all the battleships had been placed in Battleship Row, making them easy targets:

> *It [his ship] was repaired by mid-January [1942]. In October 1941, some admiral had written a big article for* Look Magazine *about how we could defeat the Japanese in two weeks. He was very, very wrong about it, but that's how optimistic people were back then. And we, we stupidly stacked*

all our battleships in a row down there for the Japanese to sink them.

The second wave of the attack began at 8:50 a.m. During this attack, the USS *Nevada* was hit by a torpedo but avoided serious damage because it was at the end of Battleship Row. The USS *Pennsylvania* was struck by bombs, causing a fire, and the USS *Shaw* was split into two pieces by an explosion. Shortly after 9:00 a.m., the attack ended, leaving more than 2,400 people

The wreckage on the USS *Downes* is shown here.

This Japanese Type A Midget Submarine was recovered in 1960. It didn't enter Pearl Harbor, as the torpedoes hadn't been fired.

dead, hundreds wounded, and the entire Pacific fleet damaged or destroyed.

HOW YOU SEE HISTORY

1. Why do you think so many people believed Pearl Harbor was a safe assignment at the time? What does this say about how people understand world events?
2. How could being far away from conflict make people underestimate the risks of war?
3. How might world events have changed if leaders had taken the early warning signs more seriously?

CHAPTER TWO

NEWS OF THE ATTACK SPREADS

December 7, 1941, was supposed to be a normal day for students across the United States. For example, Frances was at the University of Texas, getting ready for a date. But suddenly, the world changed. While people in Hawai'i faced the attack firsthand, students and families across the country learned about it over time.

Unlike today, where news is learned about nearly instantly on social media, radios and word-of-mouth were the first ways most Americans found out about things happening in the world, including the attack on Pearl Harbor. As the news about the attack spread, everyone who heard it was left in shock. Young people like Frances initially had no idea of what was happening, but they soon learned the news that the world had changed on what should have been a normal Sunday morning.

LIFE CHANGED

Pearl Harbor was attacked in the early morning local time, which was afternoon in Washington, D.C., with the time difference. The radio was mostly how Americans learned the news, and at 2:25 p.m., President Roosevelt's press secretary announced the attack. The news then spread

Scan this QR code to watch Frances describe how she found out Pearl Harbor had been bombed.

The type of bombs used in the attack are shown here.

The attack on Pearl Harbor damaged the surrounding areas, such as this military truck at Hickam Field.

rapidly through word-of-mouth as people shared the horrifying news.

Frances shared in an interview how she heard the news of the attacks:

FAST FACT

ABOUT 2,400 PEOPLE DIED DURING THE ATTACK ON PEARL HARBOR, INCLUDING 68 CIVILIANS AND 2,335 MILITARY PERSONNEL.

> *I knew exactly when Pearl Harbor was bombed. I was in college. And the reason I remember it so clearly [is because] the big thing at the University of Texas was on Sunday to have a date with somebody to go to the fraternity house. I remember pulling up in front of the fraternity house, and back then, not everybody had a car, so I was lucky my date had a car. And I pulled up in front of the fraternity house and out came one of the young men running, "Hurry, hurry, come quick. Pearl Harbor's been bombed.*

This aerial photo shows the aftermath of the attacks on December 10. Oil can still be seen leaking from the battleships.

FAST FACT

IN THE MONTHS FOLLOWING THE ATTACKS, NATIONAL BLOOD DRIVES, FUNDRAISING CAMPAIGNS, AND COLLECTION EFFORTS WERE ORGANIZED.

Roosevelt's getting ready to declare war and getting ready to speak."

And that changed our whole lives. Our whole world changed.

The day after the attack, President Roosevelt addressed Congress, calling December 7 "a date which

FUNDRAISING AND SUPPORT CAMPAIGNS

After the attack on Pearl Harbor, the American people did what they could to support the war effort and boost morale. Before the war began, there was a government savings bond program in which the federal government could borrow from citizens to prepare for the cost of war. After Pearl Harbor, these savings bonds became "War Bonds," and citizens (even children) were encouraged to purchase them with the promise of repayment with interest later.

The purchase of bonds massively increased in the weeks after the attacks, and the U.S. Treasury Department used radio advertisements, billboards, and newspapers to promote the effort. Bond drives were also promoted by popular celebrities of the time such as Gene Autry and Betty Grable, who toured the country and performed at rallies to get people to purchase bonds.

The fundraising campaigns often focused on the emotions of the war and connected the bonds to certain purchases, such as supporting wounded soldiers or funding planes. This made fundraising feel more personal, which meant people were more likely to purchase bonds. More than 85 million Americans purchased bonds, which translated to hundreds of billions of dollars in bonds.

Betty Grable, shown here, appeared at rallies with other celebrities such as Gene Autry to encourage people to buy war bonds and support the war.

Soldiers watched the attacks on Pearl Harbor and immediately rushed in to help where they could.

will live in infamy." His words united the nation and prepared them for the war they were about to enter.

NURSES WHO RUSHED TO HELP

The attack on Pearl Harbor was a source of **trauma** for those who heard the news from friends or family or on the radio, like Frances. However, it was even more traumatic for those in the immediate area, and very few have shared what happened because they wanted to forget it. Some of the stories that have been willingly shared or discovered recently are nurses' stories. Many of these nurses were in their early 20s and not prepared for what they saw that day.

Posters such as these encouraged people to purchase war bonds.

Ships were heavily damaged in the attack. The USS *California* is shown here starting to sink, while the USS *Oklahoma* in the front of the picture is mostly sunk. The USS *Neosho* is shown in the background avoiding the damage.

Nurses quickly started to help patients who were brought into the hospitals near Pearl Harbor, marking their foreheads with lipstick to help with **triage**. Those who were going to live were quickly worked on by the nurses, while those whose injuries were too severe were made comfortable and placed in a different area. Hospitals were quickly overloaded with patients, and nurses had to improvise to help them. Mess halls and other areas were set up as spaces for treatment, and the nurses' roles changed. They were trained to provide basic care, but to save as many people as they could, they provided **anesthesia** and even helped with surgeries.

Bombs fell around the hospitals, and nurses and doctors had to wear gas masks and helmets as they helped patients because the smell of the smoke was so severe. More than 80 nurses were working at three hospitals around Pearl Harbor on the day of the attack. None of them lost their lives.

Some nurses were on a hospital ship, the USS *Solace*, when the attacks started. One nurse described waking up from the ship shaking when the explosions happened, and

FAST FACT

IN JANUARY 1942, THE FEDERAL CAMPAIGN "SALVAGE FOR VICTORY" WAS LAUNCHED. IT ENCOURAGED CITIZENS TO COLLECT SCRAP RUBBER, METAL, RAGS, AND COOKING FATS, WHICH WERE USED FOR TANKS, SHIPS, PLANES, AND EXPLOSIVES.

Hospitals were also damaged. This picture was taken of damage at a naval hospital near Pearl Harbor.

she looked out her window to see smoke coming out of the USS *Arizona*. She had to quickly get dressed and report for duty.

Nurses on the USS *Solace* worked all day to help more than 130 patients, over 70 percent of which had burns. The nurses were too busy trying to help whoever they could to worry about the shaking ship, the planes flying overhead, and the explosions.

HOW YOU SEE HISTORY

1. How did the attack change everyday life for students, workers, and families?
2. How do you think hearing about the attacks on the radio or through word-of-mouth instead of seeing it instantly on TV or social media affected how people understood what was happening?
3. Frances said the attack "changed our whole world." What do you think changed first for students and families?

CHAPTER THREE

CHOOSING TO SERVE

After the attack on Pearl Harbor, the war, which had previously felt very far away, suddenly became very real. Many Americans felt like they should protect and defend their country, and military recruitment centers saw a massive amount of people rushing to join. In an interview, Charles explained how he felt when he heard the news of the Pearl Harbor attack and how he wanted to do anything he could to be a part of the war effort and defend his country.

RUSHING TO ENLIST

For many young men in America after Pearl Harbor, the decision to enlist wasn't carefully planned. It was emotional and driven by a sense of duty to the United States. Charles and many like him heard the news and, with their friends, decided that they needed to defend their country:

> *On the Sunday after Pearl Harbor, one of my friends called me, and he said, "Did you hear the radio this morning?" I said, "No." He said, "The president*

Scan this QR code to watch Charles describe what inspired him to enlist and how he tried to cheat on his eye exam to join the military.

Posters such as this one encouraging people to enlist in the military were common at the time. The posters used people's emotions about the attack to get them to join.

Fires and smoke from the explosions at Pearl Harbor could be seen from far away. These images evoked strong emotions.

just announced that our navy's been attacked out in Hawai'i and we're at war with Japan." So we *got together and decided that we would quit our jobs ... we'd go join the service and that was our aim.*

FAST FACT

MOVIE STUDIOS PRODUCED NEWSREELS SHOWING THE AFTERMATH OF PEARL HARBOR TO EDUCATE CITIZENS, SHOW THE DEVASTATION, AND RALLY PUBLIC SUPPORT FOR THE WAR EFFORT.

Sailors continued to man their boats and do what they could to fight the fires and save fellow soldiers during the attack.

FAST FACT

COLLEGES AND UNIVERSITIES BECAME HUBS FOR INFORMATION ON ENLISTING IN THE MILITARY. LINES FORMED OUTSIDE OF MILITARY RECRUITMENT CENTERS NATIONWIDE, AND MANY STAYED OPEN AROUND THE CLOCK TO HANDLE THE LARGE NUMBER OF PEOPLE WANTING TO SERVE.

After the attack, recruiting stations were overwhelmed. People waited for hours to fill out forms and speak with a recruiter, afraid that the war would be over before they could join. Others worried that they may not be allowed to join the military, especially if they had a medical condition that could disqualify them.

Not everyone who wanted to serve could serve. The military required a physical exam that tested eyesight, hearing, and general health. Many men who wanted to join the military worried that even a small medical issue would stand in their way. Charles was one of those men.

THE CHALLENGE OF MILITARY EXAMS

Even though he was determined to serve in the military, Charles worried that a minor problem—a lazy eye—would keep him out. A lazy eye is when one eye has weaker vision than the other, causing the brain to favor the stronger eye. The weaker eye generally wanders inward or outward as a result.

Charles described trying to find a way around the test so that he could join the military. His experience shows just how far some men were willing to go just for a chance to join the armed forces. They didn't know where they would be sent or what dangers they would face. They just wanted the chance to help.

In his interview, Charles described what he went through during his exam so he could join the military:

> *I've had a bad left eye all my life … a lazy eye. And I wanted to see if I could pass the eye exam. And I went down there on a non-medical day and told them my question and they said, "Let's go test him."*
>
> *I missed the line by one to passing the test. So the officer who did the testing, he said, "Why don't you go home, fill out the application, and take the test and get plenty of sleep, don't be running around all night getting drunk and whatnot, and eat carrots and celery and fruit and go to bed early and you may pass the test when you come down here."*

FAST FACT

ONE NATIONAL DONATION CAMPAIGN COLLECTED MORE THAN 5 MILLION TONS (4.5 MILLION MT) OF STEEL IN 3 WEEKS FOR THE WAR EFFORT.

ENLISTMENT INCREASE AFTER PEARL HARBOR

After Pearl Harbor, the United States saw one of the largest enlistment waves in its history. Recruiting stations in major cities stayed open late into the night, and lines of volunteers sometimes stretched for blocks. Some young men brought their parents with them to sign permission forms. Others traveled long distances just to find a recruiting office that wasn't already filled to capacity.

People from all backgrounds volunteered: teachers, factory workers, farmhands, college students, and even high school seniors who were eager to serve as soon as they turned 18. Many Americans felt that joining the military was the most direct way they could help protect their families and defend the country's freedom.

Enlistment was about more than joining the fight. It was also tied to hope and unity. Radio programs encouraged people to support the troops, and posters showing strong, determined soldiers appeared in towns everywhere. For many volunteers, enlisting created a sense of purpose amidst fear and feelings of the unknown.

Many women also joined the Women's Army Corps (WAC), the Women Accepted for Volunteer Emergency Service (WAVES) in the Navy, or the Army Nurse Corps. They took on jobs that supported the military effort, such as working in communications, repairing equipment, and providing medical care.

I followed the instructions, filled out the form, passed the written exam, and went down there for the physical … I had planned to cheat them because when I had [taken] the eye exam, the projector was on [the right side], and I thought, I know what I'll do. I'll hold the spoon [on his left side] and not over my good eye, and I'll pass it using two eyes.

When I walked in the room, he looked at me as though he recognized me, and he moved the projector [to the

Hearing of the destruction of battleships and airplane hangars, such as the one shown here, inspired people to join the military and do what they could to support the war effort.

left side]. I strained till I couldn't see the sign at all. So I flunked the eye exam … And I ended up joining the Army.

At first, Charles wanted to join the military to be a pilot. But because vision is very important for pilots, he was only allowed to join the Army. Many other recruits faced similar struggles, as a wide variety of health problems could lead to a rejection or reassignment. For example, along with poor vision, people could be rejected due to hearing issues, low weight, bad teeth, heart issues, or being too young or too old. After Pearl Harbor, people of Japanese descent were also banned from enlisting

Pearl Harbor survivors have continued to visit the USS *Arizona* memorial.

because they were considered an "enemy." However, people of Japanese descent were later allowed to join the military.

HOW YOU SEE HISTORY

1. Why do you think so many people rushed to join the military after hearing about Pearl Harbor?
2. How do you think families felt when their children decided to join the military right after the attack?
3. What risks did people face when they decided to join the military so quickly?

CHAPTER FOUR

"A DATE WHICH WILL LIVE IN INFAMY"

Before the attack on Pearl Harbor, the United States was already trying to recover from serious problems at home, including the aftermath of World War I and the Great Depression. Many people were worried about jobs, food, and security, and these challenges influenced how people felt about the idea of getting into another war. In an interview, Seymour described the feelings about going to war in the United States at the time, as well as how President Roosevelt's leadership affected those feelings.

A CHANGE OF VIEW

Many people in the United States held a view of isolationism, which is a policy that is against involvement in the wars and other political affairs of other countries. So many people held this view because the country was coming out of the Great Depression, which began in 1929 and involved very high rates of poverty and unemployment. The country was also not that far removed from World War I, which lasted from 1914 to 1918.

The combination of these two traumatic events led many Americans to believe that the country shouldn't interfere in other nations' politics or wars. Instead, they

Scan this QR code to watch Seymour discuss President Roosevelt and Pearl Harbor.

The damage to the USS *Cassin*, USS *Downes*, and USS *Pennsylvania* is shown here after the attack on Pearl Harbor.

believed that the U.S. government should prioritize focusing on internal affairs.

After the attack on Pearl Harbor and with Roosevelt's leadership, most people changed their views on involvement in the war that was already being waged overseas.

Seymour described how difficult life was at the time and how it influenced people's opinions about going to war:

Roosevelt was president at the time. And at that time the country was coming somewhat out of a depression. It was in a pretty strong depression. We had all kinds of differences of opinions on whether we should be in this war or shouldn't be in this war.

FAST FACT

AFTER THE ATTACK ON PEARL HARBOR, CIVILIANS WERE TOLD TO REPORT ANY SUSPICIOUS ACTIVITY TO PROTECT AGAINST SPIES. HOWEVER, THIS LED TO AN ENVIRONMENT OF FEAR AND THE IMPRISONMENT OF THOUSANDS OF JAPANESE AMERICANS.

This division mattered because many Americans believed the government should focus more on the problems at home rather than getting involved in another global conflict. The memory of

The Great Depression hit Americans hard. People lined up at soup kitchens, unemployment offices, and other places to get help.

President Roosevelt is shown here signing a declaration of war against Japan after the attack on Pearl Harbor.

World War I was still fresh, and many people were worried about more loss and suffering.

CONFLICTING IDEAS

As a result of the Great Depression and World War I, some people began considering extreme political ideas that promised change. Seymour explained that this created even more division and disagreement in the United States:

The Great Depression created a lot of hardship for everyone, so many Americans were reluctant to get involved in a new war.

FAST FACT

ROOSEVELT DELIVERED MORE THAN 30 FIRESIDE CHATS ON THE RADIO FROM 1933 TO 1944. DURING THESE CHATS, HE USED A CALM TONE TO EXPLAIN POLICIES, RALLY NATIONAL SUPPORT, AND CREATE A PERSONAL CONNECTION WITH THE PUBLIC.

A lot of people in government thought that fascism was the way to go. We had people who were poor and they thought communism was the way to go. We had isolationists... and they were all against the war.

These ideas reflected peoples' fear and frustration. Fascism and communism offered strict systems that some believed would solve economic problems. Fascism is a system in which a dictator controls people's lives, the government, and the economy, with the demand for loyalty to the nation above everything else. Communism is a system where all resources, farms, and factories are owned by everyone

Some people at Pearl Harbor rushed to man anti-aircraft guns.

BRAVERY AND SURVIVAL AT PEARL HARBOR

As explosions shook Pearl Harbor, sailors and civilians had to think quickly to survive. Some rushed to man anti-aircraft guns or fight fires on the ships. Others helped rescue sailors from capsized or burning battleships.

Smoke filled the air, making it hard to see, and fires spread across ships and docks. Sailors like Jim (from Chapter One) had to act fast while avoiding bombs and strafing planes. Meanwhile, medical staff worked tirelessly—one nurse, Myrtle Watson, worked for three days straight without sleep—to treat the wounded. Hospitals quickly became overwhelmed as hundreds of soldiers and civilians arrived with burns, broken bones, and other injuries.

Many people risked their lives to save others. Soldiers dove into the water to pull drowning crewmates from overturned ships. One civilian, Julio DeCastro, cut through the hull of the USS *Oklahoma* and saved 32 sailors. Rescuers faced explosives, fuel, and thick steel while trying to save everyone they could. They worked in the darkness, guided to the trapped men by their banging on surfaces.

Doris "Dorie" Miller was the first Black American to earn the Navy Cross for his bravery during the attack. He was on the USS *West Virginia*, below decks, when the first torpedo hit. He helped carry the dangerously wounded ship captain to safety and then loaded and fired the anti-aircraft gun. Because the military was segregated, he hadn't been taught how to operate it. He even stayed behind after the order was given to abandon the ship to rescue shipmates.

Soldiers rushed in to help others, even when ships were exploding and smoking. A small boat is shown here trying to rescue sailors during the attack.

together instead of individuals, which aimed to eliminate poverty, extreme wealth, and social classes. With so many different viewpoints, it was difficult to figure out a way forward.

ROOSEVELT UNIFIED THE COUNTRY

Even though there were different views on whether the United States should join the war or not, President Roosevelt believed strong leadership was necessary. In his interview, Seymour described Roosevelt as someone who could bring people together and motivate them during uncertain times:

FAST FACT

ON DECEMBER 8, 1941, PRESIDENT ROOSEVELT DELIVERED HIS SPEECH WITH THE FAMOUS LINE THAT PEARL HARBOR WAS "A DATE WHICH WILL LIVE IN INFAMY." THE U.S. OFFICIALLY JOINED WORLD WAR II ON THIS DATE.

What probably got us into the war ... was we had probably the greatest motivator ... which would be Roosevelt ... He took this divided country and at the right time, he got

President Roosevelt is shown here delivering one of his fireside chats before the attack on Pearl Harbor.

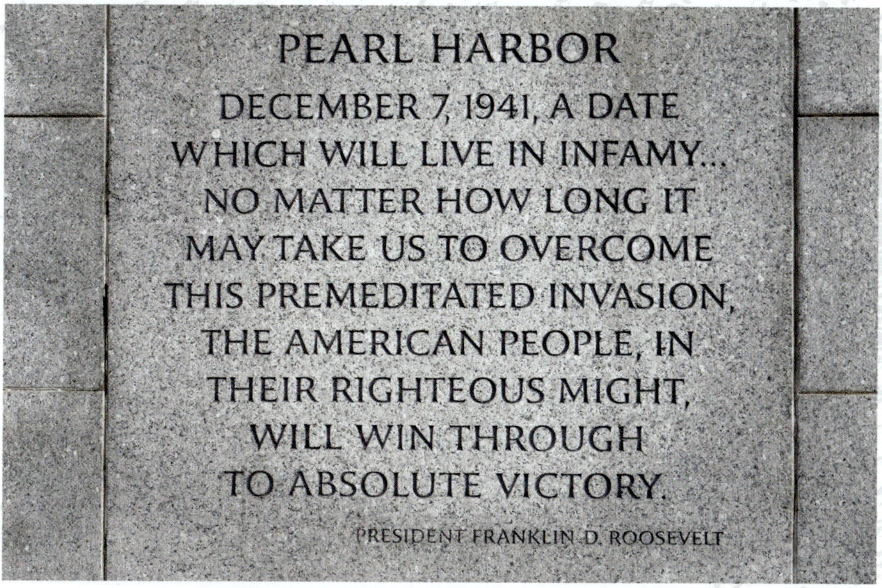

President Roosevelt's famous speech is displayed on a memorial in Washington, D.C.

> *'em all ready to say "Let's go," and that's when the Japanese hit Pearl Harbor.*

Roosevelt used speeches and radio broadcasts to explain events and prepare people for the possibility that the United States may have to act by joining the war.

Then, the attack on Pearl Harbor shocked the nation and united Americans almost instantly. Arguments about whether or not to join the war nearly disappeared, and Americans suddenly shared a common purpose.

HOW YOU SEE HISTORY

1. Do you think the fear and uncertainty after Pearl Harbor affected how people treated each other? Why or why not?
2. Why did many Americans support isolationism before the attack on Pearl Harbor? Do you agree with their reasons?
3. Why do you think some people turned to extreme political ideas during this time?

CHAPTER FIVE

THE AFTERMATH OF PEARL HARBOR

After Pearl Harbor, life in the United States changed almost overnight. Families across the country had to adjust to shortages, rationing, and new rules designed to help the war effort. Even daily routines like shopping, eating, and traveling were different. Jay was a child in school when Pearl Harbor was attacked. In an interview, he remembered how much things changed at home in just a short time.

RATIONING AND DAILY LIFE

After the attack on Pearl Harbor, families suddenly had to ration food, gas, rubber, and other essential goods. Coupons and stamps became a part of daily life, and households had to carefully plan meals and travel. Children and adults alike learned to "make do" with less and to find creative ways to support the troops overseas. Jay described how rationing impacted his family:

I remember coming home from school ... the radio was on, and they were broadcasting that Pearl Harbor had been struck. We're at war, and things changed ... There were gas coupons, rationing, and you put these stickers on your car and you were either in

Scan this QR code to watch Jay describe the changes to daily life after Pearl Harbor.

Posters used the Pearl Harbor attack and imagery such as this to encourage people to join the military and make other sacrifices such as rationing to support the war effort.

A or B or C and there were stamps to get food and stamps to get meat and my mother collected grease and gave it back to the butcher in exchange for stamps. The grease was used supposedly to make explosives somehow.

Because of rationing, many families started to grow "victory gardens," which were supposed to help add to the smaller amount of food families now had and to stretch meals even further. These gardens were community and home plots filled with plants such as tomatoes or lettuce and became a symbol of pride and dedication to the war effort.

CHANGES IN SCHOOLS AND COMMUNITIES

Schools and local communities also felt the impact of Pearl Harbor. In Hawai'i, many schools shut down immediately after the attack, with some schools having students take classes in other areas, such as homes or churches. Students had to carry gas masks and many older students joined the war effort. Schools also became centers for the community to support each other.

In Hawai'i and across the United States, students participated in bond drives, collected scraps of rubber and metal, and learned about air raid drills. Families had to navigate new safety rules and curfews, and children often heard about the war from their parents, neighbors, and teachers.

Families in Hawai'i also faced food and resource shortages because Hawai'i is an isolated island state and depends a lot on imports, which were disrupted after the attack. Meat, sugar, and canned items were strictly rationed, and families could only buy what they were allotted in coupon books. Grocery stores often had empty shelves, and families frequently worried about starvation. This led many to hoard rations such as canned ham because they were worried food shipments would end.

These changes influenced an entire generation, and many young people took

FAST FACT

SCHOOLS HELD ASSEMBLIES AND JOINED GOVERNMENT-SPONSORED PROGRAMS TO EXPLAIN THE PEARL HARBOR ATTACK AND ENCOURAGE STUDENTS TO CONTRIBUTE TO THE WAR EFFORT.

The Pearl Harbor National Memorial sits above the USS *Arizona*. The ship can be seen below the water.

THE IMPACT OF PEARL HARBOR ON THE JAPANESE

Racism against people of Japanese descent massively increased after Pearl Harbor. This led to Executive Order 9066, which allowed the military to force more than 120,000 Japanese Americans into internment camps. An internment camp is where large groups of civilians are imprisoned without trial because of their ethnicity or nationality, or because they're believed to be a **threat**. Political leaders had supported the executive order at the time because they believed, without any evidence to support it, that some Japanese Americans may act as spies.

Japanese Americans were removed from their homes on the West Coast into inland camps even though there was no reason for them to be removed. Officials claimed that these people were moved to protect national security, but many local citizens were targeted. They could only take the possessions that they could carry and then were placed in very tight areas in the camps, which were surrounded by barbed wire. Many people lost homes, businesses, and farms because of this order.

Anti-Japanese propaganda continued to depict Japanese people as lesser than other people, which created a harsh environment where racial **discrimination** was more important than a person's human rights. Those who were forced to live in these prison camps were there from 1942 until about 1946, with some camps closing down in late 1945 with the end of the war.

The effects of imprisonment lasted for many years, and in some cases, never went away. People experienced a lot of trauma and no longer trusted the government. Families were also torn apart, and feelings of trauma and distrust were passed down to children, affecting relationships and children's sense of security. Many Japanese Americans also became less involved in politics, civics, and their communities.

It wasn't until the late 1980s that a formal apology was made as well as a $20,000 payment to each surviving person who was in the camps.

on tasks that were meant for much older people, such as helping in fields, learning first aid, and participating in the sale of war bonds and rationing. While young people missed out on some normal activities, they also developed a strong sense of responsibility and patriotism.

FAST FACT

"JUNIOR COMMANDOS" WERE A NATIONWIDE YOUTH GROUP THAT SUPPORTED THE WAR EFFORT BY COLLECTING SCRAP PAPER, RUBBER, AND METAL FOR WAR MATERIALS. CHILDREN WOULD GO DOOR-TO-DOOR TO ASK NEIGHBORS FOR THESE ITEMS OR GO THROUGH YARDS AND ATTICS TO SEARCH FOR THEM.

THE PEARL HARBOR MEMORIAL

Today, visitors to Hawai'i can learn more about the Pearl Harbor attack and honor those who lost their lives by visiting the Pearl Harbor National Memorial. One of the most important parts of the memorial is the

More than 80 years after the attack, the USS *Arizona* continues to leak oil every day, which is shown here. The Navy avoids intervening to stop the leakage because the battleship is considered a memorial and they don't want to disturb the soldiers who are entombed in the wreckage.

The Pearl Harbor National Memorial has a cutout where visitors can view the USS *Arizona* below.

The concrete base of the USS *Arizona*'s gun turret is visible above water.

While most of the USS *Arizona* sunk, parts of it are still above water.

USS *Arizona*. When the battleship exploded and sunk, it wasn't removed from the harbor floor. Today, the memorial sits above the sunken battleship, allowing visitors to see parts of the ship beneath the surface when they look down into the water. Near Ford Island, the USS *Utah* was never recovered, and it remains where it partially sank. Part of the battleship is visible above the water.

Inside of the USS *Arizona* memorial, the names of those who died are carved into a white marble wall, showing that the attack wasn't just a part of history—it has affected real people and families even today.

The USS *Utah* was never recovered and part of it is still above water today.

FAST FACT

AFTER THE ATTACK, MANY CITIES PRACTICED "BLACKOUT DRILLS," IN WHICH LIGHTS WERE COVERED, STREETLIGHTS TURNED OFF, HEAVY CURTAINS USED, AND HEADLIGHTS TURNED DOWN LOW TO MAKE CITIES APPEAR DARK FROM THE AIR AND PREVENT THEM FROM BEING TARGETED.

The attack on Pearl Harbor may have happened more than 80 years ago, but the impact is still felt today. It changed the lives of the people who lived through it and changed the course of American history. By learning about Pearl Harbor, we can honor those who were affected and better understand the choices

The full length of the USS *Utah* near Ford Island is shown here.

A list of the names of those who died in the attack is carved into a white marble wall in the Pearl Harbor National Memorial.

people and nations must make in times of crisis while working toward a safer world.

HOW YOU SEE HISTORY

1. Can you find any similarities between how Japanese Americans were treated after Pearl Harbor and how other groups were treated after national tragedies or acts of war?
2. Why do you think the government encouraged children to take part in scrap collecting, bond drives, and Junior Commandos? Do you think children should be involved in war efforts? Why or why not?
3. Why is it important to have memorials like the Pearl Harbor National Memorial?

TIMELINE

THE UNITED STATES MOVES TOWARD WAR: TIMELINE OF PEARL HARBOR

- **1937:** Open warfare starts between Japan and China, resulting in the United States giving its first loan to China.
- **1939:** The United States ends its Treaty of Commerce and Navigation with Japan and starts restricting materials such as oil.
- **1939:** World War II begins. The United States stays out of it.
- **1941:** Japan enters an alliance with Germany and Italy, leading to the United States cutting off all financial relations and stopping shipments of war materials.
- **December 7, 1941, at 7:55 a.m.:** The first wave of the attack on Pearl Harbor starts.
- **December 7, 1941, at 8:50 a.m.:** The second wave of the attack on Pearl Harbor starts.
- **December 7, 1941, at 9:00 a.m.:** The attacks on Pearl Harbor end.

NEWS OF THE ATTACK SPREADS: TIMELINE OF PEARL HARBOR

- **December 7, 1941, at 2:25 p.m.:** President Roosevelt's press secretary announces the attack on the radio.
- **January 1942:** The federal government launches the "Salvage for Victory" campaign.

"A DATE WHICH WILL LIVE IN INFAMY": TIMELINE OF PEARL HARBOR

- **December 8, 1941:** Roosevelt delivers his "infamy speech," and the United States officially joins World War II.

GLOSSARY

aerial: Occurring in the air.

alliance: A group of people or countries joined together in some activity or effort.

anesthesia: A medicine that blocks pain and sensation for a short while so surgery can be performed.

anxious: Very nervous or worried about what might happen.

assault: A violent attack.

capsize: To turn so that the bottom of a boat is on top.

commerce: The large-scale buying and selling of goods and services.

deployment: To put military personnel in position for a specific purpose.

discrimination: Different—usually unfair—treatment based on factors such as a person's race, age, religion, or gender.

enlist: To engage for duty in the military.

export: An item moved from one country to another for the purposes of trade.

intense: Existing to an extreme degree.

navigate: To find one's way.

negotiate: To discuss something formally in order to reach an agreement.

racism: The practice of treating others poorly because they are part of a different race, or group of people who look alike in certain ways. This word also relates to governments and societies that allow one race to be treated better than others.

resolve: To find an answer or solution to something.

restrict: To limit or control.

strafing: A military attack where low-flying aircraft attacks targets on the ground.

tension: A state in which people, groups, or countries disagree with and feel anger toward each other.

threat: The possibility that something bad or harmful could happen.

trauma: Something that causes extreme emotional stress.

triage: The sorting of treatment to patients according to how badly they're in need of care.

FOR MORE INFORMATION

BOOKS

Allen, Thomas B. *Remember Pearl Harbor: American and Japanese Survivors Tell Their Stories*. Washington, DC: National Geographic Kids, 2015.

Favreau, Marc. *Attacked!: Pearl Harbor and the Day War Came to America*. New York, NY: Little, Brown and Company, 2023.

Katz, Susan B. *The History of Pearl Harbor: A World War II Book for Kids*. Naperville, IL: Callisto Publishing, 2021.

Messner, Kate. *History Smashers: Pearl Harbor*. New York, NY: Random House, 2021.

Owens, Lisa L. *Attack on Pearl Harbor*. Minneapolis, MN: Lerner Publications Company, 2018.

WEBSITES

History: Pearl Harbor
www.history.com/articles/pearl-harbor
Read facts, the history of Pearl Harbor, and more from the History Channel.

National Parks Service: Pearl Harbor
www.nps.gov/perl/index.htm
Explore Pearl Harbor memorials and history.

Pearl Harbor
pearlharbor.org/
Learn more about the memorial, timeline, and history of Pearl Harbor.

Pearl Harbor Attack
ww.britannica.com/event/Pearl-Harbor-attack
Read more about the Pearl Harbor attack at *Encyclopedia Britannica.*

Remembering Pearl Harbor
www.war.gov/Multimedia/Experience/Remembering-Pearl-Harbor/
View additional survivor videos, learn about the Pearl Habor battleships, view photos, and more.

INDEX

T

U

V

W

PHOTO CREDITS

Cover courtesy of the Library of Congress; pp. 7, 13, 24, 25, 27, 30, 32, 39, 40, 42, 42, 47 courtesy of the National Archives; pp. 9, 11 courtesy of the U.S. Naval History and Heritage Command; pp. 10, 14, 15, 16, 26, 38, 41, 49 Everett Collection/Shutterstock.com; p. 17 Photograph of the wreckage of the USS Downes, hit by bombs during the attack on Pearl Harbor - NARA - 306547 - cropped/ Wikimedia Commons; p. 18 Japanese Type A Midget Submarine/ Wikimedia Commons; p. 20 Benny Marty/Alamy Images; p. 21 Photograph of a machine-gunned army truck at Hickam Field, Hawaii, after the attack on Pearl Harbor - NARA -306550/Wikimedia Commons; p. 22 Pearl harbor aftermath/Wikimedia Commons; p. 23 Betty Grable - Studio portrait (1935)/Wikimedia Commons; p. 31 Wheeler Field (7 Dec. 41)/Wikimedia Commons; p. 35 Hickam Field (7 Dec. 41)/Wikimedia Commons; p. 36 Flickr - Official U.S. Navy Imagery - A Pearl Harbor survivor, salutes the Arizona memorial during a wreath laying ceremony at Joint Base Pearl Harbor-Hickam/Wikimedia Commons; p. 44 Franklin D. Roosevelt having a fireside chat in Washington, D.C - NARA - 196760/ Wikimedia Commons; p. 45 Maximin Stock/Shutterstock.com; p. 51 Mae Pon/Shutterstock.com; p. 52 (top) Phillip B. Espinasse/ Shutterstock.com; p. 52 (bottom) Andre Nantel/ Shutterstock.com; p. 53 (top) Viktor Fuchs/Shutterstock.com; p. 53 (bottom) The remains of USS Utah. (8263436887)/Wikimedia Commons; p. 54 Cucumber Key Photography/Shutterstock.com; p. 55 Michael Warwick/Shutterstock.com.

ABOUT THE AUTHOR

NICOLE HORNING is a published author of several nonfiction books for children and teens. She has her Bachelor's degree in English and a Master's degree in education. She doesn't just write for a living; she also enjoys it as a hobby. Nicole loves to collect books and read anything that sounds interesting to her. She also loves learning new things, especially historical topics. She does her best work while listening to Taylor Swift and having one of her two cats in her lap—both things happen a lot.

FIRST-PERSON STORIES OF THE

ATTACK ON PEARL HARBOR

BY NICOLE HORNING

ROSEN PUBLISHING PRIMARY SOURCE LIBRARY

ROSEN PUBLISHING

Published in 2027 by The Rosen Publishing Group, Inc.
2544 Clinton Street, Buffalo, NY 14224

Designer: Deanna Lepovich
Editor: Nicole Horning

Library of Congress Cataloging-in-Publication Data

Names: Horning, Nicole author
Title: First-person stories of the attack on Pearl Harbor / Nicole Horning.
Description: Buffalo, NY : Rosen Publishing, [2027] | Series: The Rosen Publishing primary source library | Includes index.
Identifiers: LCCN 2026006647 | ISBN 9781725342996 library binding | ISBN 9781725342989 paperback | ISBN 9781725343009 ebook
Subjects: LCSH: Pearl Harbor (Hawaii), Attack on, 1941 | LCGFT: Interviews | Anecdotes
Classification: LCC D767.92 .H676 2027 | DDC 940.5426693–dc23/eng/20260224
LC record available at https://lccn.loc.gov/2026006647

Manufactured in the United States of America

CPSIA Compliance Information: Batch #CSRYA27. For further information, contact Rosen Publishing at 1-800-237-9932.